**big & SMALL**

Original Korean text by Mi-yeon Ahn
Illustrations by Soo-jin Jo
Korean edition © Dawoolim

This English edition published by big & SMALL in 2017
by arrangement with Dawoolim
English text edited by Joy Cowley
English edition © big & SMALL 2017

ISBN: 978-1-925234-58-9
Printed in Korea

# What Can Tails Do?

Written by Mi-yeon Ahn
Illustrated by Soo-jin Jo
Edited by Joy Cowley

Some animals have tails,
but I do not have a tail.

What can animals do
with their tails?

Some animals can hang onto something.

The howler monkey hangs
from a tree by its tail.
Pouched mice hang on
to their mother by their tails.

9

Cows swish their tails to swat flies.

10

Tails can keep bugs away.

A horse wags its tail to get rid of bugs.

11

# Some animals can stand up with their tails.

Meerkats use their tails to stand tall. It helps them see far away.

A kangaroo props itself up
on its tail.

# Some animals can swim with their tails.

Killer whales wave their tails to swim.

14

**Some birds display their tail feathers
to attract female birds.**

Male birds-of-paradise have
fancy tail feathers.

Don't they
look handsome?

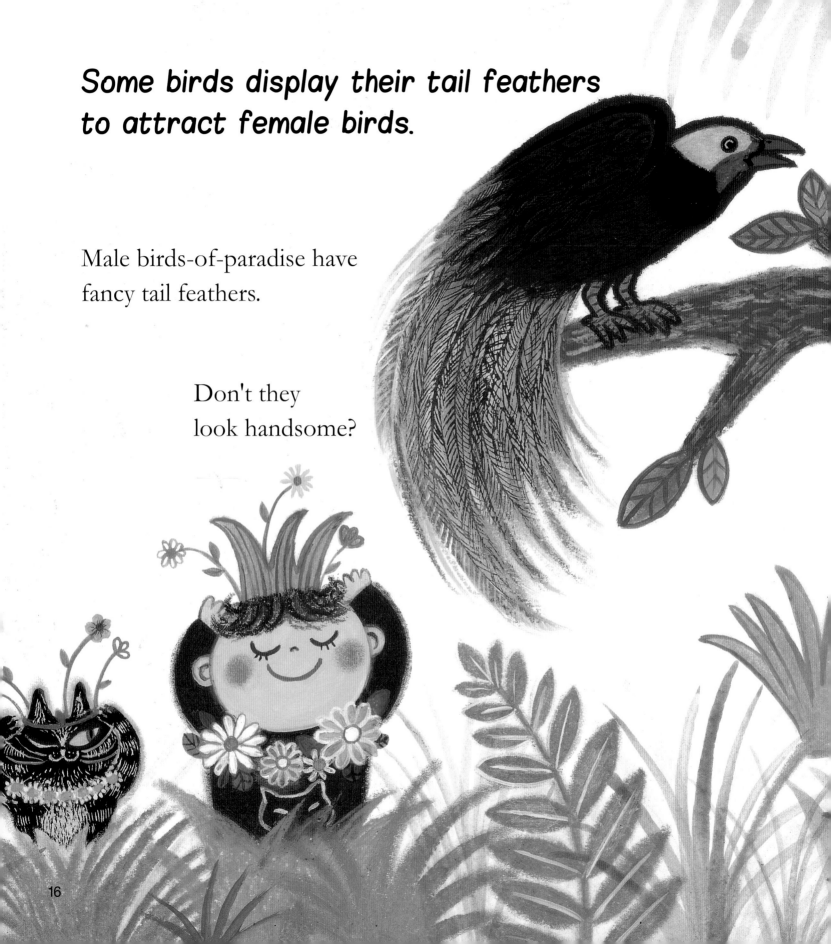

Male peacocks spread their tail feathers wide.

17

Some animals can attack or defend themselves using their tails.

A pangolin quickly moves its scaly tail to fight its enemies.

18

The crocodile swishes its heavy tail.

A rattlesnake rattles its tail to make a scary noise.

Some animals can also jump with their tails!

Dolphins jump by swinging their tail fins.

Some animals balance
with their tails.

When a tiger runs and turns, its tail sticks out. It balances the tiger's body.

The fox balances with its tail as it quickly turns.

23

Tails also help animals escape!

A salamander drops its tail to get away.
It grows a new tail later.

25

A tail can keep an animal warm.

A big anteater covers its body
with its long, warm tail.

A squirrel sleeps by wrapping
its tail around its body.

Tails dangle! Tails wave!
Tails are curly! Tails are straight!
Most animals have a tail.

# What Can Tails Do?

Animals use their tails to hang onto tree branches,
whisk away bugs, swim, jump, balance, attack and defend,
or keep warm. Find out the many things animals do with their tails.

## Let's think!

What do horses do with their tails?

How do killer whales move their tails to swim?

How does a rattlesnake defend itself?

What happens to a salamander's tail when it is being chased?

## Let's do!

Make your own animal tails! Use yarn, construction paper,
feathers, socks and cotton balls. Fill socks with cotton balls.
Make long tails with many strands of yarn. Or cut out a tail
shape from construction paper and glue on some feathers.
Tie on or tape tails to your back. See what kinds of fun tails
you can make!